To my ...

Beverley, hoping your
trip was all you expected

Love Charlie

# Charlie up a gum tree

When Johnnie's brand new football got stuck in a fork of Charlie the magpie's tree, it looked as if it would have to stay there until the wind blew it down.

The boys tried throwing stones at it then the cricket ball but it fell into Mrs Sankey's yard. She rang the policeman and they all gave up. All except Johnnie.

*For Anna*

# Charlie
## up a gum tree

E.A. Schurmann

*Illustrated by*
*Bruce Treloar*

HODDER AND STOUGHTON
SYDNEY   AUCKLAND   LONDON   TORONTO

First published in 1985 by
Hodder & Stoughton (Australia) Pty Limited
2 Apollo Place, Lane Cove NSW 2066

National Library of Australia Cataloguing-in-Publication entry
Schurmann, Ted 1917–
    Charlie up a Gum Tree
    For children
    ISBN 0 340 35775 4
    1.Title (Series: Stoat books)
A823'.3
Typeset in 16/18 pt Bembo by Griffin Press Limited, Adelaide
Printed in Hong Kong at Everbest Printing Co Ltd
Reprinted 1986

# Contents

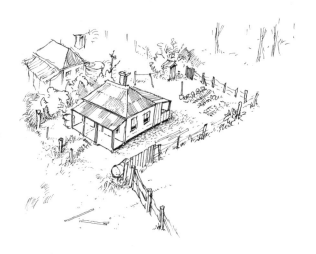

# 1   The Birthday Present

When I asked my father what a climax was, he said, after he had thought about it for a while, that it was something big at the end.

"Like the tail on a kangaroo?"

"No, I mean something big that happens at the end. Like in a story."

So if a climax comes at the end, it might seem strange that this story starts with a climax.

It was on Johnnie's birthday. Johnnie was my little brother and he was seven that day. If Johnnie was seven, I must have been eleven which means it was the year 1929. Our family had a general store in Bulla-wollock in the Wimmera in Victoria. It was called Kohlmanns Pty Ltd. My name is Willie Kohlmann.

In 1929 business was not good. Times were hard and the farmers and the business people had no money to spare.

Birthdays were among the biggest days in our year, like Christmas and Easter. I know our parents would have liked to have given Johnnie a little party for his birthday, but my mother explained to him that because times were bad, that could not be. It was all they could manage to give him a small present.

As it happened, there *was* a birthday party that day. Kevin Buller's birthday was on the same day as Johnnie's. Kevin turned twelve and had a big party. Both Johnnie and I were invited, though I thought Johnnie was lucky to be asked. He was just a little kid and there were not many little kids there.

For the first part of the party we had a game of football. We had to use a funny old ball that was only about three-quarters blown up and was all out of shape. During this game somebody knocked Johnnie over. I didn't see who it was, but I saw Johnnie getting up again and he looked very pale.

I know a lot of the time my brother was a bit of a nuisance, but I did not like to see him get bowled over and looking sad like this. I suppose he should not have mixed with bigger boys in a game of football.

After the football, because this was September and in between the cricket and football seasons, we played cricket. And after that we went inside the Bullers' house. Kevin's father was the bank manager and their house was in the same building as the bank. The party was in a big room and there were a lot of good things to eat on the table.

When we had all eaten a lot, there were party games. The last game was "Pass The Parcel", or "Mystery Parcel", as some people called it. This game started, in case you've never been in it, with the person running the party, at this party Mrs Buller, bringing in a big parcel. Inside the parcel, after a lot of layers of wrapping paper, was a prize.

Mrs Buller read out the message written on the parcel.

"To the boy with red hair."

She handed the parcel to Pinkie Meredith and Pinkie stood up and had to unwrap the parcel, then read out what was on it this time.

Pinkie read, "To the boy who likes homework."

Then Pinkie had to hand it to somebody else and that's how the game went along.

Alf Schultz got the parcel twice. The first time it said, "To the best footballer," and the other time, "To the best cricketer." Alf was not the best footballer and when he played cricket he did not even know how to hold the bat properly. But one thing he certainly was best at was fighting. The boys handing over the parcel must have wanted to keep on the right side of Alf.

The parcel, which had been very big at first, gradually became smaller and smaller, and we could tell that it must be getting near the finish, when the special prize in the middle would go to somebody lucky.

Well, at that stage the parcel was handed to

me. I stood up and was aware of all the boys sitting anxiously around me. I even saw little Johnnie's pale face as he sat peering eagerly forward.

I unwrapped the parcel and read out loud, "To the boy whose birthday it is."

Of course I didn't have much time to think about it, but I knew that this would be the prize turn. What I remembered was that it was Johnnie's birthday, so I stepped over and handed the parcel to him. I heard one of the mothers who was there helping say, "Brotherly love," and Mrs Buller herself, who had arranged the parcel, said, "Ooh!"

Johnnie unwrapped the parcel, his eyes bulging, and inside was a beautiful, new football. Everyone knew that this was meant to be the highlight of the party, with Kevin Buller getting the big present.

Johnnie looked as though he couldn't believe his luck and, although all the kids crowded around wanting to see his prize, he hugged it to himself pretty hard.

Later, as we were leaving to go home, Kevin Buller stood at the door and shook

everyone's hand and thanked us for coming to his party. When my turn came he shook my hand coldly and hardly smiled and I knew he was thinking of the football he didn't get and that he would rather have hit me on the chin than shaken my hand.

## 2   Charlie's Boundary

At home, I had to bring an armful of wood into the kitchen wood box. While I was in the kitchen I overheard my father and mother talking inside.

"Willie gave the parcel to Johnnie," my mother was saying, "and Johnnie got a football. It surprised everybody. The football was supposed to go to Kevin and be the climax of the party."

"It would have been a climax all right," my father said.

It was just after this that I asked my father

what a climax was. I also said to him, "We have a football now but we can't play in the paddock. Will you shoot Charlie for us?"

You see, beside our house and the garden and the orchard, was a fairly big paddock, which should have made a fine football ground. At the start of the football season, even though we did not have a ball then, I'd gone down to mark out a boundary line for a football oval, and to put up goal posts.

I was about halfway down the paddock when Charlie attacked me.

Along the side fence, the one furthest from the house, was a row of gum trees. These were pretty high and in one of the biggest was the nest of Charlie the magpie. Charlie generally didn't like people coming near his place and he became quite savage. He would swoop down on us when we were least expecting it, clicking his beak and giving us an enormous fright.

When I asked my father about shooting Charlie, he said, "Instead of that, let's go down and try to sort things out with Charlie."

So we went down to the paddock, with

Johnnie trailing along behind us. Everything was all right until, when we were about in the middle of the paddock, suddenly from out of the gum tree came Charlie, flying straight at us. He swished very near to us, clicking his beak. It was a most frightening experience.

My father turned around quickly and so did I and we walked back a little way. Then my father stopped.

"That's very interesting," he said.

I wouldn't have thought that exactly.

He stood there for a while, then he walked forward a little way and Charlie came out of the tree again. Then, as my father turned and came back to me, Charlie flew back into his tree.

"You were talking about boundary lines," my father said.

"Yes. We need a boundary line for the footy ground."

"Well Charlie has his own boundary line."

"Where is it?"

"Charlie's the only one who could tell you that. But where we are standing is over his boundary. I suggest you scratch a line along here somewhere and keep your football ground on the safe side of it. You are lucky, having a paddock big enough to make two football grounds."

I thought they would be pretty small football grounds.

"Don't you think it'd be better to shoot Charlie?"

"No," my father said. "You don't shoot magpies. Only the policeman could do that." Then, "Look at Johnnie! Come back, Johnnie, Charlie will chase you!"

"No," I told my father, "Johnnie's quite safe. Charlie doesn't chase the little kids."

"Great Scot! I mean, fancy that," my father said.

## 3    The Cricket Match

For some reason Johnnie wanted his football to stay new. My father had it blown up tightly for him, but Johnnie would not let me or anyone else touch it.

Anyway the football season was just about over, so I got out the cricket things and arranged a game on the next Saturday. A lot of kids turned up, including Kevin Buller, who probably expected to have a few kicks of the new football. My best friends, Doolie Walcott and Jack Coventry, came too, and a few others. We picked sides.

Johnnie and young Adrian Leopold were

hanging around and my mother had told me very strictly that whatever we played, Johnnie and Adrian must be allowed to play, too. Well, although I had Doolie on my side, the other team seemed to have the best players and, to make it worse, they had one more man than us.

"I'll tell you what," Kevin Buller said, "to give your side a better chance, you can have both the little kids. That way you have one more man than us, but that's fair enough. All right, toss for innings."

The cricket pitch, from which we had cut off all the grass, was at the house end of the paddock, out of Charlie's area. There was always a wicketkeeper or backstop, of course, and behind him was a patch of high, thick grass which had never been cleared. This stopped the ball from going over Charlie's boundary. No matter how fast a ball was travelling, the thick grass would always stop it.

Well this day, Kevin Buller won the toss and his side batted first and made a fairly good score, which we set out after when it was our turn to bat.

But Doolie and Jack Coventry and I were all out and there were still about six runs to get and the only batsmen we had left were Johnnie and Adrian, the little boys.

Johnnie never made any runs. In fact the bat was nearly as big as he was and he couldn't move it properly. But he took block,

although he didn't know what that meant, and faced up to Kevin Buller's bowling.

Kevin went back and took a long run and I could see he was going to send down a fast one, and I thought maybe he's thinking of that football that Johnnie won.

It was a fast one all right that bounced high off the dirt pitch. It whizzed past Johnnie's ears and past the wicketkeeper, Pinkie Meredith, too. Then it flew right over the patch of high grass and landed on the other side and sped on into Charlie's territory.

Pinkie set off after it.

I yelled out to Johnnie and Adrian, "Run! Run like mad!"

Johnnie dropped the bat and set off for the other end and Adrian did likewise.

Kevin shouted, "Hurry up, Pinkie. Don't let them get two!"

But Pinkie had stopped dead. As he neared the ball, Charlie had come out of the gum tree and swished around his head. Pinkie howled and held his hands up over his face.

"Pick up the ball and throw it!" Kevin Buller shouted.

Pinkie wasn't watching the ball. He was watching Charlie diving straight down at him. Charlie clicked his bill and fluttered up, then turned and attacked Pinkie again. Pinkie was waving his arms and shouting loudly at Charlie.

Johnnie and Adrian were running up and down the pitch, counting their runs, and we were clapping them. Kevin Buller set off after the ball himself in disgust. Charlie saw him coming and changed his direction, making Kevin stop dead in his track. Then there was the click of a bill which sounded as though it might have been on Kevin's head.

Kevin and Pinkie retreated until Charlie stopped chasing them. The little lads were still going up and down the pitch as fast as their legs would carry them.

"That's twelve they've run," Doolie said. "We've won. That's enough."

That was the end of the game. I sent Johnnie, who was still puffing pretty hard after all that running, into Charlie's territory to recover the ball. Johnnie trotted along and picked it up while Charlie just sat in his tree and watched him as though he and Johnnie were firm friends forever.

I didn't feel so bad about Charlie, either.

# 4  Mrs Sankey

Often on those Saturday afternoons, when it got a bit hot or we felt we needed a spell from a game, we would sit in the shade of one of the gums and have a talk. I used to shoo Johnnie away at times like this.

My father had told me very firmly that I must make sure that none of the boys who came to our place was ever cheeky to Mrs Sankey. She was our neighbour and lived next to our paddock. Her house was set well back from the road. A stone's throw back, in fact.

We found out for sure that it was a stone's throw one day when Doolie Walcott had been to our place.

It was on a Sunday afternoon. Doolie had come up to see me and found nobody at home because we were all at church. He realised this when he looked over at the church—another stone's throw from our place. He saw buggies with their horses tied up there, and cars in the shade, and he could hear people singing.

Doolie said it wasn't right to have church in the afternoon. I explained to him that Lutherans often had afternoon church, so that they wouldn't have to go out at night. Anyway, at the time Doolie felt so frustrated about it that he picked up several stones and let fly and the first two landed on the church roof.

The singing stopped suddenly and Doolie thought he had done it and that he had better be on his way before they came out looking for him. He still had a couple of stones and, as he was passing Mrs Sankey's place, he decided that her iron roof would be a good place to get rid of them. So he tried his arm again and the yonnies landed fair on Mrs Sankey's place and made a lot of noise as they rattled down.

Then Doolie saw Mrs Sankey's front door opening and knew it was time for him to leg it again. He waited until he thought church would be over, then came back to our place. I still wasn't home, but this time Doolie waited for me. When I came home he had to wait longer still while I changed out of my good clothes.

We spent the rest of the afternoon together until it was time for him to go home.

Doolie had forgotten about the stones he had thrown earlier, but Mrs Sankey hadn't. She saw him on his way home again through her window and quickly got out her broom, then sneaked out to her front garden and waited behind some shrubs. As Doolie came past she sprang out and began flaying him with the broom.

Doolie was taken completely by surprise and copped a few whacks before he decided to run. Only then he found he could not

better Mrs Sankey's speed and she chased him along the road for a long stretch, keeping up with him and whaling into him with the broom at the same time.

This wasn't the only time that we saw how fast Mrs Sankey could run.

One day I was inside when my father came in, laughing. He went into the kitchen and I heard him telling my mother what he was laughing at.

"I just saw Mrs Sankey going to her clothes-line with a basket of washing, when Charlie swooped down at her. She dropped the basket and ran. You should've seen her. She ran like a hare."

"Poor lady. You shouldn't laugh."

"Next thing she was back with her broom to challenge Charlie."

He laughed a bit more about it.

"Don't you let the children hear you laughing at Mrs Sankey," my mother said.

My father had a good sense of humour and often made jokes out of things. But he usually did this without even smiling, always keeping a straight face. It was unusual for him to laugh like this and I thought it must have been funny all right. So I hurried out to see if it was still happening.

I was surprised to see Mrs Sankey, at her clothes-line and wearing a big sun hat, hanging out her washing quite peacefully. There was no sign of Charlie at all.

## 5  Charlie in Trouble

That long path from the road to Mrs Sankey's door proved a bit of a problem for some of the tradesmen who had to deliver things to her. I think she had had arguments with all of them from time to time.

She said that Mulga Bloor, the butcher, had kicked her cat. Mulga denied this. He said he had just swung back his boot to show the cat what would happen to it if the wrong kind of person came along. He always encouraged people's pets to get out of the way for their own good.

Mrs Sankey said she had seen her cat go

flying over the paling fence, but Mulga Bloor said it was just getting out of his way and went over the fence under its own steam. He would never deliberately harm an animal, Mulga Bloor the butcher said.

After that Mrs Sankey made Mulga come to her house the back way. He had to climb the fence of the paddock behind her place and he had made a little track from there to her back door.

I said at our tea table one night that Mulga Bloor climbed over Mrs Sankey's back fence just as though there was no barbed wire on top of it. My father said that he didn't think Mulga Bloor would even feel barbed wire. He said Mulga was tougher than his own meat.

After a while Mrs Sankey had another argument with Mulga, about his meat this time, and now he didn't even go to her place the back way.


Although my father had laughed about Mrs Sankey running away from Charlie the magpie, it turned out that she took it very seriously.

One day when Charlie chased her, she went to her telephone and rang Tom Cole, the policeman. She told him he must do something about the very dangerous magpie that lived in our gum trees. When she put down her telephone and went out of the back door, Charlie came for her at once. So she went right back inside and rang Tom Cole again.

After a few more phone calls the policeman felt he would have to do something about it.

I was there the day he drove up and stopped his car at the end of our paddock. I saw him get out of the car, then reach in and pick up his gun. I hurried down to him.

He said, "G'day, Willie. Where's this magpie that keeps attacking people?"

"He's all right, Mr Cole. So long as you keep out of his territory."

"Show me his territory."

I pointed down past the cricket pitch to the bottom gum trees. Tom strode off.

I said, "There are other maggies there. Mind you get the right one."

"Willie, I don't like doing this. Magpies are protected birds. I'll only shoot the wild one."

He turned back and kept walking. I started to follow him, but then changed my mind. Johnnie had come out and stood beside me.

"He's going to shoot Charlie!" Johnnie said. Big tears started coming out of his eyes, although I knew he was trying to stop them.

I watched Tom Cole, who looked very tall. He wore his policeman's uniform with his big, shining black helmet. I thought Charlie would really like to peck that helmet. The

buttons on Tom Cole's uniform were all shiny and new looking, too. With his rifle in his hands, he was looking up at the trees.

I looked up at the trees, too, and suddenly I saw Charlie sitting up there. Johnnie reached up and grasped my hand. Normally I would have brushed his hand away but I didn't do that today. I held on to it tightly.

Tom Cole walked along until he was right under Charlie's tree. Then he stood there looking up at Charlie, while Charlie looked down at him.

After a time Tom Cole walked back again.

"There was a magpie there but it wasn't the right one," Tom Cole said.


Next morning I was late getting to the breakfast table. I put milk on my weeties and reached for the cream. My mother always scalded some of the milk to get this lovely cream off the top. But this morning there was hardly any cream left.

"Johnnie's taken all the cream!"

"He's taken half of it," my mother said.

"You still haven't learned to share things with your brother."

I suppose I wasn't used to Johnnie having weeties for breakfast. I said, "He's the one who can't share things. He should take a smaller share."

"Be quiet," my mother said.

My father changed the subject. "I believe you had the policeman to see you last night?"

"He came to shoot Charlie. Only Charlie didn't go him."

"Didn't go for him," my mother corrected me.

"Why didn't he go—go for Tom Cole?" I asked my father.

"Charlie's a sensible bird. He knows that a policeman must be respected. You will notice Charlie always picks his mark."

"He always picks me," I said.

"That's because you're not on his list of people he respects," my mother put in.

"I'm on his list," Johnnie said.

I thought Johnnie was a bit cocky that morning. He was safe from the magpie and he had a lot of cream on his weeties.

33

# 6   Doctor Eaglehawk

After that it began to look as though Charlie really did have some kind of a list of people he would not go for. Johnnie and the policeman were on it, and I soon found out that the doctor was on the list, too.

Our doctor's name was Doctor Eaglehawk. He was a very friendly man who drove a single-seater Ford. At least he drove his Ford when he could get it started, though sometimes it would not go, no matter how hard he cranked it. When his car wouldn't start, Doctor Eaglehawk would ring Peter Watson at the garage and Peter would go over to his place and turn the crank handle once. Then the car would always start and Doctor Eaglehawk would say:

"I just can't seem to get the knack of it."

"Well, every man for his own trade," was Peter Watson's answer. "I mean, I wouldn't know how to cut anyone's leg off. Not until I'd had a bit of practice at it."

Doctor Eaglehawk sometimes thought it was quicker to visit a patient on foot instead of going to all the trouble of cranking his car. You could always see him coming because of the hat he wore. It was a soldier's hat from somebody, I think Doctor Eaglehawk's brother, who had been in the war. The hat had big feathers in it. When they wore out, Doctor Eaglehawk put in new feathers of various colours. Lots of the kids, when they found a big feather out of an eagle or a cockatoo or a pelican, would give it to Doctor Eaglehawk.

Once my father said, "The doctor puts a new feather in his hat every week."

"And calls it macaroni," my mother said.

"What does that mean?" I asked her.

"I haven't the slightest idea," she said.

Well, what happened was that one day Doctor Eaglehawk's car broke down on the road right at the bottom of our paddock. I heard this happen. I mean, one minute I could hear the noise of the car going along and then there was a bit of a bang and then silence. I ran to the paddock to see what had happened and there was Doctor Eaglehawk getting out of his single-seater car.

I stood and watched him. He cranked it for a while and then he gave up and began walking. I knew he was coming to our place to ring up Peter Watson. He climbed through the back fence and suddenly I remembered Charlie. I thought it would be a bad thing for Charlie to go for the doctor and maybe even peck him.

I started to run down into the paddock to warn Doctor Eaglehawk but, when I crossed his boundary, Charlie swished at me, giving me a terrible fright. I turned round and shouted, then Charlie came at me again and I had to run back over his boundary.

He flew into his tree and I saw that Doctor Eaglehawk was still walking along, wearing his hat with the big feathers in it. I waited for Charlie to go for him but the magpie just sat there. That was when I knew he respected Doctor Eaglehawk.

The doctor came up to where I was standing.

"Hello Willie. I'm going up to your place to use your telephone. I just came past the

place where you had your bonfire last Guy Fawkes."

"Hello doctor. There was a magpie up in the tree watching you. He goes for some people, but other people he respects and you are one of them."

"He's a very wise magpie," Doctor Eaglehawk said.

That evening, when my father came home for dinner, my mother told him that when Doctor Eaglehawk used our telephone, before he had a chance to ask for Peter Watson's number, the girl at the post office told him that a lot of people had been ringing up for him and she gave him all their names.

My mother also said that Doctor Eaglehawk did not take off his hat when he came inside, which could be a bit of a shock for sick people.

## 7  Johnnie's Football

I suppose it took another three or four days before I realised that Charlie did not have a list after all.

It came to me one morning as I watched Mrs Sankey go to her clothes-line, hoping that Charlie would swoop at her and make her run like a hare. But she went about calmly hanging up her washing and Charlie did not come. Yet she wasn't on any list, because Charlie had gone her in the past. I mean gone for her.

Then suddenly I saw what it was. Mrs Sankey was wearing her big sun hat. She often wore it when she went out into her backyard, whether or not the sun was shining.

That was the secret! The hats. I thought of Doctor Eaglehawk with his hat with all the feathers in it. And of Tom Cole, wearing his shining black helmet.

I was a bit excited and ran down to the side fence as Mrs Sankey came up from her clothes-line.

"Hello Mrs Sankey."

"What do you want?"

"It's your hat that frightens Charlie. Not your broom."

"What on earth are you talking about? Charlie who?"

"Charlie the magpie."

"Why do you call him Charlie?"

"It's his name."

"Good heavens, who gave it that name!"

"I don't know. Nobody, I think. It just came."

"What did you say about my hat?"

"You're all right as long as you wear your hat. I mean Charlie won't chase you when you have your hat on."

"Utter nonsense. I think you're being cheeky."

"No, not this time, Mrs Sankey. I—"

"Yes you are. Go away or I'll be out after you with my broom."

"Don't forget your hat, Mrs Sankey."

She hurried inside then and I hurried away.

All this time, Johnnie's football, though blown up tightly, had not been used. It still looked its new shiny tan colour and sat on top of the cool safe on our back verandah. I used to look at it and think how good it would be to bounce it a bit and to kick it, even just a little kick in the backyard. But Johnnie said it was going to stay new for a while yet.

I suppose I couldn't complain about him wanting to keep it looking new, because I was doing exactly the same thing with my cricket ball.

Last year my mother had a long talk to me about the bad times. She told me not to expect anything big at Christmas. Then my Grandpa gave me a brand new cricket ball, all shining and red, with its parts sewn together with very strong thread.

This ball looked so beautiful that I had never used it for playing cricket. I knew that if I did it would soon lose its bright red colour, as it was hit along the ground and into gum trees and got barbed wire scratches on it.

But my mother had told Johnnie and me that we would have to take our things off the cool safe soon, because the weather was starting to warm up and she would have to get the cool safe going straight after Guy Fawkes day. To do this she always cleared everything off the top and poured buckets of water into the top part. The water went down the sides of the cool safe on flannel strips and dripped into a bucket. Every time one of us went past in the summer months we were supposed to empty the bucket back into the top part.

One day at school there was an argument about cool safes. Somebody said they were called cool safes because they kept everything inside them cool. Then someone else said that was not the reason at all. The "cool" part of the name was short for Coolgardie, which was where these safes came from. The argument got very strong and would have gone on for a long time except that Alf Schultz settled it. He said he would fight anyone who didn't agree with his side of the argument. I've forgotten now which side he was on.

## 8　Caught in a Gum Tree

As it happened, there was no Guy Fawkes at our place that year.

There were two reasons for this. One was that there was no money for fireworks, and the other was that I had not built a bonfire. Normally we would have had a bonfire on Guy Fawkes night, even without crackers and sky rockets and other things to let off, but the bonfire had to be in the paddock, well away from the house, and of course I could not go down there because of Charlie. Usually I made a bonfire from old dead branches which I would drag across the paddock from under the gum trees.

It was on the day after what would have been Guy Fawkes that I saw a swaggie coming along the road at the back of our place. There were always swagmen about in those days and we used to call them "swaggies" for short. They would carry a rolled-up bundle of blankets or rugs on their backs with a sugar bag tied to the bundle and a billy dangling down.

My mother said that, on average, a swaggie came to our place asking for something to eat every few days. They were a bit of nuisance, but she always gave them a parcel of things —usually some tea and sugar, and perhaps part of a loaf of bread or some meat.

But this swaggie wasn't coming to our place, because I could see him climbing through the fence at the back of Mrs Sankey's. He had put his swag and things on the ground and had taken off his hat, I suppose because he was calling on a lady. As soon as he started to walk along the track to Mrs Sankey's back door, Charlie swooped at him.

I could see that the swaggie got a terrible fright. He started hitting into the air where Charlie was, or where he thought Charlie was, but Charlie kept diving at him from new angles. In the end the swaggie hurried back, climbed through the fence again and picked up his swag.

This fence was not outside Charlie's boundary and he kept swooping at the swaggie, who waved his hat at Charlie, which made Charlie come at him all the harder.

About this time my mother told Johnnie that

now he really must move his new football from the cool safe. She was almost ready to pour water on top of the safe.

So one day Johnnie asked her to hand the football down to him. He hugged it pretty hard because he was more fond of it than ever, even though it had never been used. He stepped off the verandah into the backyard and bounced the ball on the ground. The noise of the bounce sounded really good, so he bounced it again.

"Can I have a bounce?", I asked.

Johnnie thought about it, then tossed the ball to me. I walked around the yard, bouncing it.

"I'll kick it to you, Johnnie."

"No, I want first kick."

So I walked across and gave him the ball, then stepped back for him to kick it to me. It went off the side of his boot, but that was counted as the first kick, so I ran and grabbed it.

Word got around at school that Johnnie was using his new football and on the next Saturday some of the kids came up to our place to have a kick. Before we thought about starting a proper game, we played kick-to-kick for a while. That means a group of kids at each end kick the ball from one side to the other.

This was very enjoyable, especially with the new football, and we were all so wrapped up in the game that we must have forgotten about Charlie.

We were playing at the house end of the paddock, out of his territory. Then someone kicked the ball pretty hard and it went over the heads of the kids at the other end. Doolie Walcott had to chase it and he ran right into Charlie's territory. Suddenly, Swish!, Charlie came at Doolie just as he was picking up the ball.

Doolie yelled at Charlie and Charlie dived at him again. Then Doolie picked up the ball and saw Charlie flying up into a gum tree. Without stopping to think, Doolie kicked the football as hard as he could in the direction of Charlie. The ball flew into the top of the gum tree and there it stuck.

## 9   Throwing Stones

We all stood just over Charlie's boundary line and looked up at the ball in the tree. Charlie sat in the next tree, wiping his beak.

Doolie said the only thing to do was to throw stones at the ball to knock it down. So we gathered up all the stones we could find and let fly, but none of them made much impression.

Because it was November and not really the football season any more, I had brought the cricket things into the paddock, too, in case we got tired of football and wanted a game of cricket later on. I thought the cricket ball might be a better thing to throw at the football than stones.

I had first throw but I was a bit off target. The ball hit the main trunk of the tree about halfway up and flew off sideways, right into Mrs Sankey's place. It bounced a couple of times, then rolled up to her back door.

We saw the door open at once. Mrs Sankey came out, picked up the ball and went back inside. I climbed through the fence, hurried into her place and knocked on the door. Mrs Sankey opened it and glared at me.

"Well?" she said.

"Please can I have my ball back, Mrs Sankey?"

"No."

"But I didn't mean—"

"No. Now go away and stop bothering me or I'll telephone Mr Cole."

I went back to the others despondently. Now there was no football to kick and no cricket ball, either. Nobody else knew about my new cricket ball, and anyway I wasn't going to bring it out just yet.

Doolie said the only thing to do was to try again to knock down the ball with stones. Our first job, he said, was to gather up all the stones we could find. So we spread out and started stone hunting. We had to go a good distance, because we couldn't go into Mrs Sankey's paddock or over Charlie's boundary. But in the end everyone came back carrying a lot of stones.

It was decided that only those who were good at throwing should have shots at the football. Even so, there were some pretty wild throws. I noticed that some of Doolie's stones went right over the top of the tree into Mrs Sankey's back paddock, where Charlie had chased the swaggie.

This went on for some time. Jack Coventry hit the football once and it moved, but then it just fell back into the fork where it was cradled. We were all excited about that and were telling Jack it was a god shot, when we saw the car stop on the road at the house end of the paddock. Everyone recognised Tom Cole's blue Chevrolet.

Mr Cole got out of his car and came through the fence and we all stood and waited as he walked up to us. He wore ordinary clothes today and an ordinary hat. He looked very stern.

"What's all this stone throwing going on?" he said.

We had not thrown a stone since he had driven up, so we knew that somebody had told on us. Of course we knew who that somebody was.

"Our footy's up the tree," Doolie said. "We've been trying to knock it down."

Tom glanced up at the football.

"Well, you should watch where you kick it. Now you'll have to wait for a windy day to blow it down. But no more throwing stones over the fence. Understand?"

"Yes, Mr Cole," we said together.

"Right." He turned to go.

"Mrs Sankey took our cricket ball," I said quickly.

"What do you mean, she took it?"

"She picked it up and took it inside."

"Picked it up where from?"

"From—from near her back door. It rolled there accidentally."

The policeman pondered.

"I think you'd better forget about your cricket ball for a while."

He moved away again. My father was coming into the paddock to see what was wrong. When he met Tom Cole, he started talking to him. They walked up to our house together.

"Your father is going to be arrested," Doolie Walcott said.

Afterwards, when I went inside, Mr Cole

was still there having cups of tea with my father and mother.

That night, after Johnnie had undressed, my father brought Johnnie's trousers into the living room. He began taking stones out of the pockets, one by one, stone after stone. In the end there was an enormous pile on the living room table, all out of Johnnie's pockets.

"No wonder the policeman came," my mother said.

## 10   A Fall

The next Sunday was like most other Sundays, although I could not help noticing that Johnnie was sad about his football and kept looking at the place on top of the cool safe where his ball had been all this time.

On Monday morning I woke up early, put my clothes on and decided to go down to the paddock just in case there had been some wind overnight and the ball had come down. When I got there I had a real shock. What I saw was little Johnnie, trying to climb the tree after his football.

I raced down and hardly thought about Charlie coming, though maybe it was too early in the day for him. I stood under the tree. Johnnie was about a quarter of the way up and he was stuck there.

"You're too high," I shouted. "Come down at once."

Johnnie looked down over his shoulder. I saw him look up again and I'm not sure which way he tried to move, but his foot slipped off the branch and he fell out of the tree. As he came down, part of his body hit against the lowest bough, then he somersaulted over and fell the rest of the way so that his head hit the ground first.

"Johnnie!" I yelled.

His eyes were shut and he didn't hear me. I said, "Johnnie boy!" and leaned right over him. Then I lifted him up. Although he wasn't heavy, not at first, I was puffing as I started to carry him up to the house.

"Johnnie," I said, "can't you talk?" But he didn't. Then I saw little bubbles coming out of his mouth, a bit red with blood. His head rolled back and his eyes opened a little, but

they weren't like his ordinary eyes, they were just white. They closed again and Johnnie was quite still. The only noise was my loud puffing.

I hoped my mother was up and when I got near the house I was really pleased to hear her in the kitchen.

"Mum," I sang out, "come here!" She called back, "What's the matter?"

"I've got Johnnie!"

Then she came out and lifted Johnnie from me. "Oh, my little boy!" she whispered.

"He fell out of the tree. He was after his football."

"Open the door for me, Willie. Quickly."

My mother carried Johnnie in and put him down on his bed. Then I heard her ringing Doctor Eaglehawk. Then she came out and told me to get my own weeties, which I did, and I was careful not to have more than half the cream.

Doctor Eaglehawk arrived soon with his bag. He took his hat off and went into the bedroom and I could hardly hear the voices. Everything was very quiet.

Somehow I thought of the day when Johnnie had been born, in this very house. It was over seven years ago, but I could just remember it. Doctor Eaglehawk had come and my father told me to be very quiet so I wouldn't disturb the new baby. I remember that there was a noise like a nanny goat in the distance and my father said:

"He's having a little cry."

Now I sat there eating my weeties and

wishing that Johnnie would start to cry again, a little cry or as loud and as long as he liked.


I collected my schoolbag and went out. At first I thought if I waited around, Doctor Eaglehawk might give me a lift as far as his place in his car. But then I realised it might take him a good while to start it and I'd be later than ever to school, and I was going to be late enough as it was.

But I'd have a good excuse for being late. I could tell everybody about Johnnie falling out of the tree.

## 11  Kevin to the Rescue

It wasn't until the morning playtime that I had all the kids around me listening to my account of how Johnnie had fallen from a great height in the gum tree. I told them how his eyes had opened once then closed again, and how he was still very much unconscious.

Everyone stopped talking as I talked about Johnnie. Johnnie would have been pleased, if he hadn't been unconscious, to know that he had so many good friends at school.

I hurried home that afternoon and saw the doctor's car outside our place and I thought that meant things were very serious. Only when I came in did I learn that the car was still there from this morning because it wouldn't start.

I asked about Johnnie and my mother said he was sleeping peacefully, but I knew that what she really meant was that he was still unconscious. I was not allowed to go in and look at him.

During the night I woke up and a light was on. I heard my mother moving about the house, so I knew things were still serious.

Next morning I got up early and thought I would have another look in the paddock, just in case the ball had blown down from the gum tree. This time when I looked into the tree I had another shock. In fact, it was a very big shock at first because I thought Mrs Sankey was up in the tree. Then when I had a closer look I saw that it wasn't Mrs Sankey, it was Kevin Buller wearing Mrs Sankey's hat.

The whole thing flashed across my mind very quickly. Kevin Buller had known the ball was still up in the tree. He had never forgotten that he was supposed to have had that football for his birthday and now he thought this was a good chance to get it. So he had got up early and come to our place and on the way had borrowed Mrs Sankey's hat, which always hung on a peg just outside her back door, so he would be safe from Charlie while he climbed the tree.

I decided to wait to see whether Kevin was able to get the football or not. If he did get it, I would stand there with my hands on my hips as he came down. If Charlie didn't come, I would fight Kevin and get back the football.

But as I watched him climbing up the tree and heard a small branch break off under his foot, so that he quickly had to grab another branch, I was suddenly very frightened. I watched Kevin Buller struggling up the tree and remembered how Johnnie had fallen. I was more scared than ever and turned and ran back to the house.

Inside my father had just come out of the bedroom in his pyjamas and dressing gown.

I said quickly, "Kevin Buller is up our gum tree after the football."

"Great Scot!" my father said.

That was all he said. I thought he would have said something about what could be done about Kevin, but he just went on to the bathroom.

Then my mother came from Johnnie's room.

"Johnnie is awake," she told me. "He wants to know if his football is still in the tree."

I stood there with my mouth open. I said, "I'll go and look." Then I dashed outside again and started racing towards the paddock. I stopped suddenly when I saw Kevin Buller coming up to the house with the football under his arm.

"Hello Willie," he said, when he saw me. "I've got Johnnie's football for him. I thought I should get it because I'm good at climbing trees."

My mother and father came out to see what was happening.

I said, "You know Kevin, don't you?"

"I thought it was Mrs Sankey," my father said.

Kevin realised he still wore Mrs Sankey's hat and he took it off quickly.

"Here's Johnnie's football," he said.

My mother said, "Kevin, you take it in to him. It will make him feel a lot better, I'm sure."

Kevin put Mrs Sankey's hat on top of the

cool safe, which still didn't have water in it, and he went inside carrying the football. I followed him in and for some reason we were both walking on tiptoes.

Johnnie looked very pale on the pillow, but his eyes were wide open again, with the blue parts clear in the middle. He saw Kevin and the football and he smiled and looked happy.

"Hello Kevin. Hello Willie."

"Here's your ball," Kevin Buller said. "From up the tree."

Johnnie took the ball and cuddled it to himself and put it right under the blankets.

My mother came in and said quietly, "You must both go now. You will have cheered Johnnie up tremendously."

We went out. Outside the back door Kevin reached for Mrs Sankey's hat and he saw my new cricket ball on the cool safe.

"Wow, what a beauty!" he said. "Is it yours, Willie?"

"Yes," I said.

"We'll be needing that, seeing Mrs Sankey took our other one. I hope you'll let me have first bowl with it. A fast bowler can really make a ball like that swing, you know, Willie."

I let him touch it for a while. He put it back and said he must hurry home for breakfast. After he had gone I saw he had left Mrs Sankey's hat there.

## 12   Friends and Neighbours

I told my father about Mrs Sankey's hat.

"Well, you'd better take it back to her," he said.

"She won't understand. I'm sure she'll ring up Mr Cole again. Do you think you could call in and explain things to her?"

My father thought it over. "I'd rather explain it to Tom Cole," he said.

My mother came out and said happily, "Johnnie is asking for his weeties."

I sneaked down to Mrs Sankey's place with her hat. I needn't have worried. She was not up yet, so I carefully and quietly hung the hat back on its peg. I thought that perhaps I should start wearing some kind of big hat myself when I was in the paddock.

As I raced home again, I saw that though Mrs Sankey was not up, Charlie was. He sat watching me from his usual gum tree and I was careful to keep outside his territory.

I am not sure exactly when I had my big idea. But some time at school during that day I thought of it. I hurried home after school quicker than I ever had before.

My mother said, "Stop puffing. You've been running hard. Go in and say hello to Johnnie, then come back and I'll give you a piece of cake."

I thought my mother looked a lot better herself today.

I came back and said, "Johnnie's still got his football in bed."

"Yes," my mother said, "it's made him very happy. A real tonic. He's starting to remember everything that happened. You've got your cricket ball back, too."

"My— who—"

"Mrs Sankey brought it back. She came to see Johnnie."

"Mrs Sankey!"

"Yes, she brought him some custard and you're going to have to eat it. She explained that she kept the ball for a few days just to teach you a lesson about not throwing things into her place."

"She rang up Tom Cole as well."

"That was about the magpie. She thought you were throwing stones at the magpie."

"You mean she— she—"

"Didn't I tell you? Mr Cole told us on Saturday when he was here that Mrs Sankey phoned him because she thought all the boys were throwing stones at the magpie in the tree. She reminded Mr Cole that magpies are protected birds."

"But she hates Charlie!"

"No, she does not. She loves him. She told me all about him today. She said she has discovered that Charlie is quite safe so long as she wears a hat. But what is most important, the other day he chased a swaggie who was coming into her place. She says Charlie is very good to have about when he keeps undesirable characters away and it will be a pity when he calms down and stops chasing people ... There's nothing wrong with your cake, is there, Willie?"

"No, I—I'm kind of surprised. About Mrs Sankey ... It's real nice cake."

Then I remembered the idea I'd had and told my mother about it.

"Yes, I think it's a good idea, too," she said. "Would you like me to wrap it up for you?"

She took the new shining red cricket ball

and found a little cardboard box that it just fitted into and made a neat little parcel. No one would guess there was a cricket ball inside it, which made it a kind of mystery.

"When you give it to Kevin," my mother said, "thank him from all of us."

I took the parcel and set off towards Kevin Buller's place. As I walked along I felt excited about everything. After a while I started to run.

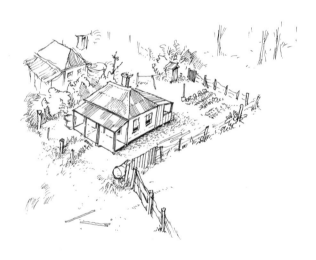